STATIONS
of the
CROSS

with the
Eucharistic
Heart
of Jesus

Apostleship of Prayer
William Prospero, S.J.
Edited and with an introduction
by James Kubicki, S.J.

AVE MARIA PRESS AVE Notre Dame, Indiana

Imprimi Potest

Very Reverend Thomas J. Lawler, Provincial Wisconsin Province of the Society of Jesus

Scripture texts in this work are taken from the *New American Bible, revised edition* © 2010, 1991, 1986, 1970 Confraternity of Christian Doctrine, Washington, DC, and are used by permission of the copyright owner. All Rights Reserved. No part of the *New American Bible* may be reproduced in any form without permission in writing from the copyright owner.

The publisher gratefully acknowledges the Sisters of St. Francis of Assisi in Milwaukee for permission to use the images of the Stations of the Cross in their St. Joseph's Chapel and Fred Leonard for his photography of them.

Founded in 1865, Ave Maria Press is a ministry of the United States Province of Holy Cross.

www.avemariapress.com

Paperback: ISBN-13 978-1-59471-638-6

E-book: ISBN-13 978-1-59471-639-3

Cover and text design by David Scholtes.

Photography by Fred Leonard.

Printed and bound in the United States of America.

Foreword

Fr. William F. Prospero, S.J., was born on the feast of St. John Vianney, patron of all priests: August 4, 1965. I was his vocation director in 1987 when he applied to enter the Society of Jesus, and at various times over the years I was his spiritual director. I was privileged to see his profound love for the Sacred Heart of Jesus, the Eucharist, and the Blessed Virgin Mary.

These reflections, which Fr. Will shared with me some years ago, are an expression of that love. During Holy Week 2014, while Fr. Will was suffering from kidney cancer and chemotherapy, which compromised his immune system and allowed an incipient fungal pneumonia to attack, I offered them on the weekly Apostleship of Prayer radio show. A listener was so moved that he asked me to get them published. I asked Fr. Will's permission to edit them for publication, and he agreed. Ave Maria Press also saw their value and graciously agreed to publish them.

Fr. Will lived these reflections. He walked the Way of the Cross with Jesus, surrendering himself to the incomprehensible and perfect will of the Father. He made his final surrender on a feast of Mary, the woman of his life, the one whom St. John Paul II called "the Woman of the Eucharist." Fr. Will died on September 8, 2014.

These reflections are intended for private rather than public or group use. They are the fruit of eucharistic adoration and are an ideal prayer for holy hours and visits to the Blessed Sacrament.

James Kubicki, S.J.

Introduction

The Second Vatican Council taught that the Eucharist is "the source and summit of the Christian life" (*Lumen Gentium*, 11, quoted in *The Catechism of the Catholic Church*, 1324). The Church gathers at the Eucharist to celebrate the saving mysteries of our redemption, those mysteries that make the Church. We believe that the celebration of Holy Mass makes present—in a real, yet unbloody, way—the passion, death, and resurrection of our Lord and Savior, Jesus Christ. Such a profound mystery of faith is difficult to take in. So we savor each moment of our Lord's life, death, and resurrection by taking time to ponder the events that led to our salvation.

This meditation on the Stations of the Cross provides a way to appreciate what Jesus did out of love for each of us. Nothing is more insulting to our Lord than when those who profess faith in him take for granted what he did and what he continues to do at each celebration of the Eucharist.

In walking with Jesus through his Way of the Cross, we pause to reflect on what he did for us. As we appreciate these sacred moments of our Lord's passion and death, we prepare ourselves to more deeply appreciate the power of his resurrection.

Opening Reflection

At the time he was betrayed and entered willingly into his Passion, he took bread and, giving thanks, broke it, and gave it to his disciples, saying: "Take this, all of you, and eat of it, for this is my body, which will be given up for you."

The Roman Missal, Eucharistic Prayer II

Jesus lived these words; his whole life was a "eucharist," a thanksgiving offering to God. As I look upon the suffering Christ in this Way of the Cross, I remember these words that he spoke at the Last Supper, words that are repeated at every Mass. I ask him to make my heart like his so that I can become a eucharist for the world.

Jesus gives up his body, his heart, his very life for my love. He is extreme in his desire for me. He wants me to know how much he loves me, and he goes to such great lengths to communicate his love to me. But this extreme offer of love is frightening. I know I do not deserve it, and I falsely think I must do something to measure up to it. I despair in my ability to properly receive our Lord's abundant love for me, so I follow from a safe distance. I easily become indifferent and ungrateful for the gift he offers to me in the Blessed Sacrament.

Just as the serpent was lifted up in the desert to heal all who looked upon it from the serpent's bite, so too all who look upon the Crucified One in faith are cured of the "bite" of sin (see Nm 21:9, Jn 3:14). I will pray this Way of the Cross looking upon the Crucified One once again, calling to mind and heart the dramatic events of Christ's passion and death. I do this so I can enter more fully into the celebration of the Holy Mass, which makes present in a real way these saving events.

Prayer: Thank you, Lord Jesus, for every moment of your passion, offered for the salvation of the world. Increase my awareness and appreciation of the wounds you suffered for love of me, and help me to gratefully offer myself back to you. Amen.

I

Jesus Is Condemned to Death

Jesus said to him in reply, "What do you want me to do for you?"

Mark 10:51

I adore you, O Christ, and I bless you,

Because by your Holy Cross you have redeemed
the world.

The enemies of Jesus want to kill him because they do not understand his teachings. Jesus' friends abandon him because they are afraid of those in power. Jesus is alone in his suffering. Being misunderstood causes conflict among people every day. Misunderstandings can lead to judgment, separation, condemnation, violence, and even death. Even very good people experience the frustration of misunderstanding and its effects. Good communication is the only answer.

Pride and selfishness stifle good communication. An open, gentle, and humble heart facilitates good communication. Jesus, personally unaffected by original sin, communicates his truest self perfectly. He never hides his thoughts and feelings. He freely yet prudently communicates his identity and mission by word and action. Jesus so perfectly communicates himself that millions have come to know and love him over the centuries.

In addition to communicating himself perfectly, Jesus also perfectly receives communication from others, making dialogue real. Practicing the art of listening, he listens attentively to his Father in prolonged periods of prayer. He listens humbly to the needs of others, giving them what they most need. Jesus is not a mere dispenser of divine grace; through human faculties, he discovers the deepest needs of the person before him, and then he responds accordingly.

Jesus wants me to be an expert in dialogue with God and others. Being open and humble enables me to hear God's Word and obey it. In my petitions to God, I express my deepest needs as I know them to a God who knows me perfectly. By suffering the indignities of the Cross, Jesus proves his desire to communicate his love to me. He desires no less from me in return so that I may enter into an authentic dialogue that leads to our communion.

In the first part of the Eucharist, the Liturgy of the Word, Jesus speaks to me. Then I share my desires and needs with him in the Prayers of the Faithful.

Prayer: Jesus, meek and humble of heart, help me to invest myself in the art of good communication, understanding that bad communication can condemn innocent people. Help me to improve my communication by listening and responding to your Word and the words of others. As you so freely communicate yourself to me in the Eucharist, help me to freely give myself back to you, strengthening the bonds of love made present by Holy Communion.

Heart of Jesus, present in the Most Blessed Sacrament,

I offer myself with you for the salvation of all.

Jesus Carries His Cross

He was spurned and avoided by men, a man of suffering, knowing pain . . .

Isaiah 53:3

I adore you, O Christ, and I bless you,

Because by your Holy Cross you have redeemed the world.

Many experiences formed the heart of Jesus. The sacred scriptures found a home in his heart as he prayed them alone, with his family, in the synagogue and the Temple, and among friends. However, nothing formed the Sacred Heart of Jesus more than his experiences of suffering: his struggles to accept the limitation of his own humanity as evidenced by forty days of temptation in the desert, the indifference and ingratitude for his works of mercy, the rejection and misunderstanding of the Good News that he proclaimed, and the lack of visible "success" in his ministry. Jesus was a man of great joy bringing the Good News to all, yet he was also a man of suffering, acquainted with infirmity.

When Jesus accepted the Cross, he was well acquainted with it. It fit well on his shoulders. The cross symbolizes the sin of the world that Jesus lovingly takes upon himself. Each step weakens Jesus' body but strengthens the resolve in his heart. Jesus willingly accepts this suffering because he is obedient to the Father's request that he show how much he wants to forgive our sins and reveal love.

Jesus wants to share his saving mission with me: "Whoever wishes to come after me must deny himself, take up his cross, and follow me" (Mt 16:24). Only through the cross can I share in Jesus' saving mission. The cross is the way God forms my stony heart to be like his. The more stone on my heart, the more deeply must the cross penetrate my heart. In his disciples, God wants hearts of flesh, worthy vessels of his love.

Crosses come to me every day through bodily weakness or ailment; my lack of talent, intellect, or creativity; the death of a relative or friend; an illness; a job loss; a conflict; a failure; a fault; or a vice or a sin I cannot shake. Identifying my daily crosses and offering them back to God forms in me a "priestly heart" that offers to God spiritual sacrifice on behalf of others. Lovingly accepting the cross in my daily life for the benefit of others pleases God while cultivating a priestly heart. My baptism makes me a sharer in Jesus' priestly mission.

Prayer: Lord Jesus, help me to identify the crosses in my life as opportunities to live out my baptismal call to offer myself as a sacrifice pleasing to the Father. Make my heart like yours, never complaining when the cross comes my way. Help me to spread the effects of your redemption by uniting my sufferings with the sacrifice of the Mass being offered throughout the world.

Heart of Jesus, present in the Most Blessed Sacrament,

I offer myself with you for the salvation of all.

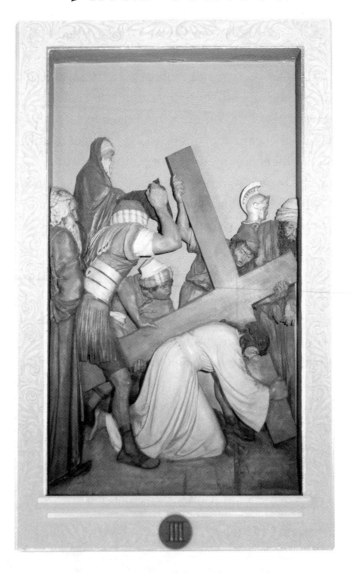

Jesus Falls the First Time

For we do not have a high priest who is unable to sympathize with our weaknesses, but one who has similarly been tested in every way, yet without sin. So let us confidently approach the throne of grace to receive mercy and to find grace for timely help.

Hebrews 4:15–16

I adore you, O Christ, and I bless you,

Because by your Holy Cross you have redeemed the world.

Jesus falls under the heavy Cross, which overcomes his weakened body. Jesus' heart falls in disappointment. The weight of the ingratitude and indifference toward his mission finally overcomes him. His heart aches with frustration. Jesus remembers how carefully he communicated the teachings of the kingdom of God. He remembers how much effort he put into listening to people's concerns and into healing and helping them. All this seems a waste now as he lies facedown on the ground.

Yet Jesus does not despair. His aching heart grasps for the promise of his Father—a promise that somehow still holds true. He picks himself up and continues on the way.

How easily my heart falls. I fall under the weight of the smallest temptation. I grasp for what does not belong to me. I easily despair when things don't go my way. I complain at the smallest inconvenience. I have a heart of stone. I ignore the blessings of God and fail to believe his promises.

The Eucharist is nourishment that gives me strength to persevere in facing life's challenges and the temptations that come my way. The Sacred Heart of Jesus, present in the Eucharist, gives me the courage and hope to keep going when I feel weak and overwhelmed.

Prayer: Jesus, change my heart! Make it strong in difficult times. Open my heart to receive faith; help me trust in your promise and your strength. Fill my heart with hope in you, not in my own accomplishments or power. Fill my heart with pure love so that I may desire you alone in all things.

Heart of Jesus, present in the Most Blessed
Sacrament,

I offer myself with you for the salvation of all.

Jesus Meets His Sorrowful Mother

Mary is a *"woman of the Eucharist" in her whole life. . . .* Mary, throughout her life at Christ's side and not only on Calvary, made her own *the sacrificial dimension of the Eucharist. . . .* Mary is present, with the Church and as the Mother of the Church, at each of our celebrations of the Eucharist. . . . In the Eucharist the Church is completely united to Christ and his sacrifice, and makes her own the spirit of Mary.

St. John Paul II, *Eccelesia de Eucharistia*

I adore you, O Christ, and I bless you,

Because by your Holy Cross you have redeemed
the world.

Jesus said, "I came so that they might have life and have it more abundantly" (Jn 10:10). Mary lived life to the full. Living life to the full does not mean indulging oneself as the world around us teaches. Living life to the full means living every moment in the heart of God. Mary lived in the heart of God as she humbly received God's Word and bore it to the world. Every moment of every day, she discovered new meaning as she meditated on God's Word, which became flesh within her. As she discovered the face of God in her Son, she came to know herself in the heart of God.

As Jesus walks the Way of the Cross, he recalls pleading with his disciples in the garden to "keep watch with me" (Mt 26:40). He remembers how they could not stay awake to suffer with him in his anguish. His Blessed Mother hears the cries of Jesus' lonely heart. She comes to him, unafraid of the crowds, the soldiers, and the utter evil of the situation. Mary's strong motherly presence breaks through the barriers of fear and evil to comfort Jesus' broken heart, giving him the strength needed to fulfill his mission.

Mary breaks through difficult situations to be with me in my suffering. Human suffering attracts the attentive heart of our Blessed Mother. Her motherly care cannot be stifled by evil. Her Immaculate Heart intensely suffers Jesus' passion and continues to suffer my passion with me. She shows me how to find meaning in my sufferings by uniting them with the sufferings of Jesus, which bring salvation to the world.

I do this every time I participate in the celebration of the Mass. The bread and wine, placed on the altar, represent me. They become the Body and Blood of Christ. As he offers himself to the Father for the salvation of the world, so I offer myself with him.

Prayer: Sorrowful Mother, help me to know my suffering as a share in the suffering of your Son. Keep me close to his heart that as I share in his suffering I might share in his joy. Amen.

Heart of Jesus, present in the Most Blessed
Sacrament,

I offer myself with you for the salvation of all.

Simon Helps Jesus Carry His Cross

But we hold this treasure in earthen vessels, that the surpassing power may be of God and not from us. We are afflicted in every way, but not constrained; perplexed, but not driven to despair; persecuted, but not abandoned; struck down, but not destroyed; always carrying about in the body the dying of Jesus, so that the life of Jesus may also be manifested in our body.

2 Corinthians 4:7–10

I adore you, O Christ, and I bless you,

Because by your Holy Cross you have redeemed
the world.

The soldiers make Simon help Jesus carry his Cross. The Cross blindsides an innocent bystander. A cross commonly surprises me at the most inconvenient times as it did Simon. How do I deal with unexpected crosses? My common reaction is complaining or self-pity. Jesus wants me to surrender all self-pity and complaining, trusting that the cross serves to purify me so that I can trust in God more than in my own strength. With Jesus, I trust that God will be faithful to his promises to the end.

Every cross, no matter how small, can unite me more intimately to the suffering Jesus. Jesus looks gratefully at Simon, who grudgingly accepts an undeserved burden. Simon quickly rejects Jesus' gracious advances, grumbling in self-pity. Eventually, as Simon begins to understand that Jesus didn't deserve the burden either, he realizes that they are together in spirit, suffering similar yet unique injustices. As he walks close to Jesus, carrying his Cross, Simon experiences a transformation. He begins to realize that Jesus suffers a much greater injustice than he, moving his attention away from himself toward Jesus. And yet Simon notices that Jesus does not complain or resist but is intent on getting to the place of execution. Simon senses something meaningful and powerful about to happen. He senses he is part of a very important plan. Seeing this, Simon experiences courage and purpose to assist this just man in his mission. Suffering alongside Jesus moves Simon out of himself to experience new meaning. When I come to know that Jesus' heart suffers for love of me, I am changed. I realize that my suffering has a meaningful purpose in God's heart.

Prayer: Lord Jesus, help me to unite my daily sufferings with the offering of the Mass, where you, through your priest, offer your Body and Blood for the salvation of the world. Soften my heart, and make it like yours. Give me a priestly heart ready to offer sacrifice for your greater glory and honor. By the power of your grace, transform my weakness, showing me how power reaches perfection in weakness.

Heart of Jesus, present in the Most Blessed Sacrament,

I offer myself with you for the salvation of all.

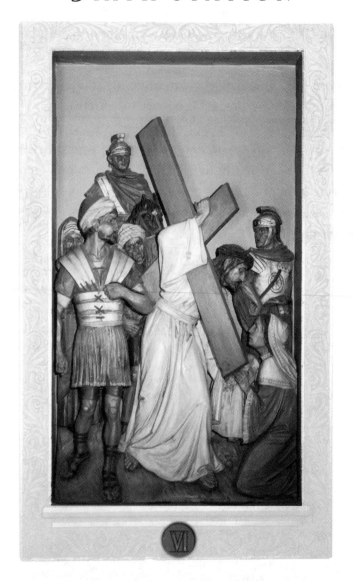

Veronica Wipes the Face of Jesus

Hear my voice, Lord, when I call;
    have mercy on me and answer me.
"Come," says my heart, "seek his face";
    your face, Lord, do I seek!
Do not hide your face from me;
    do not repel your servant in anger.
You are my salvation: do not cast me off;
    do not forsake me, God my savior!

Psalm 27:7–9

I adore you, O Christ, and I bless you,

Because by your Holy Cross you have redeemed
    the world.

In the midst of Jesus' agony in the garden, God sent an angel to give him comfort. Now Simon of Cyrene and Veronica give physical and emotional comfort to the suffering Jesus, each according to his and her unique gifts. With her womanly sensitivity, Veronica attends to Jesus' face, wounded by physical abuse. In so doing, she attends to Jesus' heart, wounded by the sins of the world.

The face of Jesus offers much to contemplate. We can learn much from viewing the face of another. Faces tell about people's states of mind, their hopes and joys, and their sufferings. The human face is the visible expression of the human heart.

What does Jesus' face look like, apart from being bloodied and beaten? What kind of look did he give to Veronica? Gratitude? Relief? Or maybe invitation? Perhaps Jesus invited Veronica to share his mission. Her kind act did not end at that moment. It was motivated by mercy, which she experienced from Jesus and which he now invites her to share with others. He calls her to be, as her name indicates, a true image of mercy for others.

I experience the merciful presence of Jesus in the Eucharist. Here I encounter the suffering, dying, and risen Jesus, who takes away the sins of the world and who feeds the hungry and gives comfort to the sorrowful. As I receive Jesus, I must do as Jesus did. I become what I receive and am transformed into an instrument of God's love and mercy in the world.

Prayer: Lord Jesus, you show yourself to me in those who suffer. Help me to recognize you in every suffering person I encounter. Move my heart to compassion so I might comfort all who are in need of your mercy.

Heart of Jesus, present in the Most Blessed Sacrament,

I offer myself with you for the salvation of all.

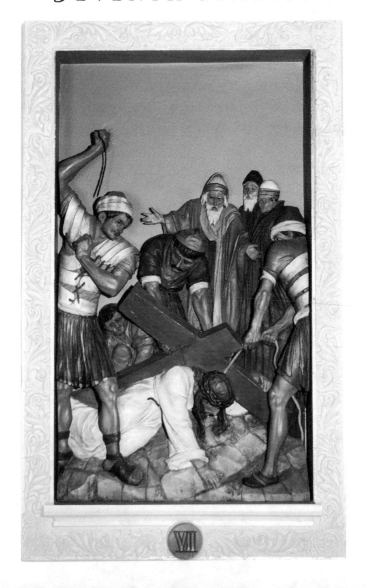

VII

Jesus Falls a Second Time

Amen, amen, I say to you, whoever believes has eternal life. I am the bread of life. Your ancestors ate the manna in the desert, but they died; this is the bread that comes down from heaven so that one may eat it and not die. I am the living bread that came down from heaven; whoever eats this bread will live forever; and the bread that I will give is my flesh for the life of the world.

John 6:47–51

I adore you, O Christ, and I bless you,

Because by your Holy Cross you have redeemed
the world.

As Jesus falls, he is face down on the ground once again. He remembers the promise of his Father, who is ever-faithful. Jesus relies on the Father's promise, alive in his heart. He shows radical trust in the midst of abject suffering. The words of scripture are alive in Jesus' heart, sustaining him when life makes no sense. Jesus picks himself up, surrendering his entire future into the hands of God.

Jesus told the woman who had been suffering from hemorrhages for twelve years, "Courage, daughter! Your faith has saved you" (Mt 9:22). Jesus commonly told people to "be not afraid." Jesus went out to people who were afraid, who did not know whether they could endure more suffering. Fear stifles faith; courage, in the midst of suffering, builds up faith.

In the midst of my suffering, there is a temptation to fear that God will abandon me to misery. It is particularly difficult to trust God when I am down on the ground, unable to look up. Jesus wants to come to me and give me courage.

Jesus comes to me in Holy Communion. I receive the same Jesus who experienced human limitation as he fell to the ground. Jesus is truly the "bread come down from heaven," falling to the ground to nourish me for the journey.

Prayer: Lord Jesus, how easily my heart gets discouraged by suffering. Suffering makes me feel abandoned by you. Help me to find you in my weakness, trusting in your mercy. At Holy Mass and Eucharistic Adoration, I meet your merciful love coming to me from your most Sacred Heart.

Heart of Jesus, present in the Most Blessed Sacrament,

I offer myself with you for the salvation of all.

JESV
S NAZARENVS
REX
VDAEORVM

VIII

The Women of Jerusalem Weep over Jesus

But Zion said, "The LORD has forsaken me;
　　my Lord has forgotten me."
Can a mother forget her infant,
　　be without tenderness for the child of her womb?
Even should she forget,
　　I will never forget you.
See, upon the palms of my hands I have engraved
　　you. . . .

Isaiah 49:14–16

I adore you, O Christ, and I bless you,

Because by your Holy Cross you have redeemed
　　the world.

The women weep because the one they love suffers. They love Jesus because he sincerely gave himself to them. He gave them the Word of life and fed them in ways that truly satisfied their hearts. He honored their natural gifts as women, helping them to know their true dignity before God and men. He freed them from oppressive attitudes by reaching into their hearts and communicating to them that they were "bone of my bones and flesh of my flesh" (Gn 2:23) and telling them, "My sister, daughter, and mother! I honor you and I love you as my equal in all things human." In his suffering, Jesus draws those who love him closer to his heart. And through this love, disciples find healing.

The women of Jerusalem cling to Jesus in their hearts, finding meaning from his powerful presence. His presence is irresistible to those who believe his words. In the same way, the Holy Eucharist draws me to Jesus. Jesus' presence, alive in me, speaks to me. He gives me loving words that heal and bring new life. The words of scripture come alive and change me, making me desire Jesus all the more. How much do I desire Jesus as he is present in the Holy Eucharist?

Prayer: Jesus, you reveal to me the truth about myself—that I am loved with the greatest love the world has ever known. As I draw close to you in your passion and death, as they are made present in the Holy Eucharist, feed me with the knowledge of my true dignity. Teach me to imitate your free and total offering of yourself in your passion and death, made present at every Eucharist. Open my heart to receive your gift of love in Holy Communion that I may become what I receive.

Heart of Jesus, present in the Most Blessed
Sacrament,

I offer myself with you for the salvation of all.

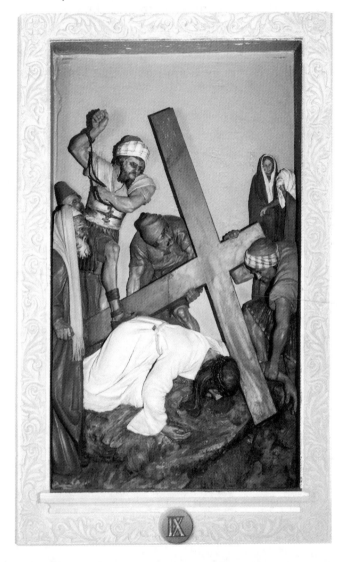

IX

Jesus Falls a Third Time

Jesus answered them, "The hour has come for the Son of Man to be glorified. Amen, amen, I say to you, unless a grain of wheat falls to the ground and dies, it remains just a grain of wheat; but if it dies, it produces much fruit."

John 12:23–24

I adore you, O Christ, and I bless you,

Because by your Holy Cross you have redeemed the world.

For the third time, we see Jesus falling to the ground, a sign of his impending death. The heart of Jesus falls as well, wondering how much more he can take, offering himself once again into the Father's hands, which he cannot see or feel. Jesus teaches me in his suffering.

At this stage in the Way of the Cross, Jesus shows me that death happens throughout life. In living every moment of life to the fullest, in completely giving himself away, and in dying to his own will and interests, Jesus prepares for death. His whole life is a dying to self, a giving away of his heart to the Father and to others. In these final moments of life, Jesus is well prepared. All these dyings prepared him now for these final moments, his surrender on the Cross.

Every celebration of Holy Mass is a falling down for Jesus. By becoming the bread of life, he once again makes himself vulnerable, exposing himself to more abuse, misunderstanding, indifference, and ingratitude. This does not stop him. Love compels him. He continues to give his Heart away, freely and without reserve, bearing fruit in humble, fertile hearts that are close to the ground.

Prayer: Lord Jesus, as you fell to the ground like a grain of wheat, help me to fall with you in my failings and sufferings. Help me to trust in the Father's will as you did, knowing that wheat must be ground before becoming bread for the life of the world. Teach me your Way of the Cross, which you experienced your entire life. Made one with you in the Holy Eucharist, help me to suffer and die for the good of others.

Heart of Jesus, present in the Most Blessed
    Sacrament,
I offer myself with you for the salvation of all.

Jesus Is Stripped of His Garments

The Blessed Sacrament was exposed, when Jesus Christ appeared to me. He was a blaze of glory— his five wounds shining like five suns, flames issuing from all parts of his human form, especially from his divine breast which was like a furnace, and which he opened to disclose his utterly affectionate and lovable Heart, the living source of all those flames. . . . He disclosed his divine Heart as he spoke: "There it is, that Heart so deeply in love with the human race, it spared no means of proof—wearing itself out until it was utterly spent! This meets with scant appreciation from most of them; all I get back is ingratitude—witness their irreverence, their sacrileges, their coldness and contempt for me in this Sacrament of Love."

The Autobiography of St. Margaret Mary

I adore you, O Christ, and I bless you,

Because by your Holy Cross you have redeemed
the world.

People wear clothing for protection from the elements, to enhance appearance, and to protect from lustful eyes. Clothing provides security for the human heart, which can be mistreated if not properly guarded. Clothing helps provide healthy boundaries for appropriate human interaction in a fallen world. Jesus' nakedness, however, exposes him to both greater abuse and to good. His nakedness makes him more vulnerable and hence more accessible to people. Jesus' external nakedness expresses the nakedness of his Sacred Heart, exposed for the world to abuse or to love more easily. My natural inclination is to move away from someone who loves me so intensely as to suffer the indignities that Jesus suffered for love of me. But Jesus wants to eliminate all barriers to my communion with him.

Of what barriers do I need to be stripped? What fears prevent my full exposure to Jesus? In Holy Communion I receive the Real Presence of Jesus Christ. Does Jesus receive in return my real presence, or do I try to hide parts of myself or my day from him?

Prayer: Jesus, help me not to be indifferent to or ungrateful for the extremes you went through to show your love for me. As you allowed your body, and thus your heart, to be exposed, showing your love for me, move me to open and expose my heart to you. Remove all barriers that hinder my communion with you. Draw me to your exposed heart in times of Eucharistic Adoration, where you are exposed for the world to love or to ignore or to abuse. Help me devote myself to loving you in the Holy Eucharist that I might more sincerely love you in the poor, the unborn, and all those exposed to unjust structures of evil. Amen.

Heart of Jesus, present in the Most Blessed Sacrament,

I offer myself with you for the salvation of all.

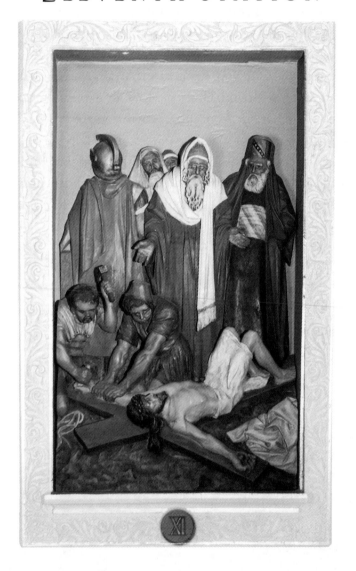

Jesus Is Nailed to the Cross

In you, LORD, I take refuge;

   let me never be put to shame....

Into your hands I commend my spirit;

   you will redeem me, LORD, God of truth.

Psalm 31:2, 6

I adore you, O Christ, and I bless you,

Because by your Holy Cross you have redeemed
   the world.

From his first days on earth, Jesus learned to trust the Father's plan. Soon after Jesus' birth, his parents fled with him into Egypt at the threat of King Herod. Jesus learned very early that being on the road helps one to trust in God's care, especially when driven by the threat of evil into foreign lands. Jesus lived the words of Psalm 31 every day of his life. As Jesus' hands are nailed to the Cross, he yet again surrenders his life into the hands of the Father.

Jesus wants me to entrust my life into the Father's hands as he did. We are all on a journey under the threat of evil. Entrusting my life into the hands of the Father requires a daily examination to see where in all the events of my day I either neglected the Father's care for me or surrendered myself to it. As I become aware of God's daily gifts and offer thanks, and as I become aware, in a spirit of repentance, of my selfishness and abuse of God's gifts, I will grow in my relationship with God.

Am I not amazed at what Jesus did for love of me?

Am I not amazed at what Jesus does every day for me in the Holy Eucharist?

Prayer: Lord Jesus, as bread must be broken to be shared, so you must be broken to be given to your friends. Help me to imitate your Way of the Cross, so that my heart, broken and offered with your heart, might give new life to the world.

Help me to see in this cycle of suffering the paschal mystery made present in the Holy Eucharist and in my life.

Heart of Jesus, present in the Most Blessed
Sacrament,

I offer myself with you for the salvation of all.

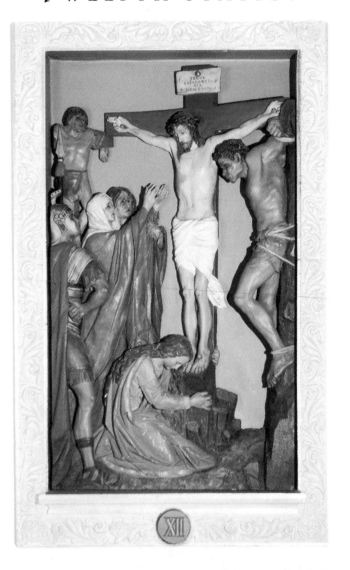

Jesus Dies on the Cross

But when they came to Jesus and saw that he was already dead, they did not break his legs, but one soldier thrust his lance into his side, and immediately blood and water flowed out.

John 19:33–34

I adore you, O Christ, and I bless you,

Because by your Holy Cross you have redeemed the world.

Blood and water gushed forth from the heart of Jesus moments after his death, signifying the very life within him poured out for love of all. Jesus emptied himself completely in these final hours of passion and death and even after death when his heart was pierced open and emptied itself.

Early Christians believed the water and blood symbolized the two great sacraments of the Church: Baptism and Eucharist. From the pierced and broken heart of our Savior comes the very substance that makes new Christians, builds up the Church, forgives sins, and renews creation.

With Mary, our Blessed Mother, and the beloved disciple, traditionally identified as John, I stand before the Crucified and Pierced One, contemplating the mystery. John was the only apostle who stood under the Cross that day. Where did he get the courage to do so?

He received courage and strength from the Eucharistic Heart of Jesus. On the previous night, at the Last Supper, John drew close to that heart as he rested his head on Jesus' chest. At that supper, he also heard and saw what I experience at every Mass: Jesus "took bread, blessed and broke it, and gave it to his disciples, saying: 'Take this, all of you, and eat of it, for this is my Body, which will be given up for you.' In a similar way, taking the chalice filled with the fruit of the vine, he gave thanks, and gave the chalice to his disciples, saying: 'Take this, all of you, and drink from it, for this is the chalice of my Blood, the Blood of the new and eternal covenant, which will be poured out for you and for many for the forgiveness of sin. Do this in memory of me'" (*The Roman Missal*, Eucharistic Prayer IV).

The Eucharistic Heart of Jesus gives me, as it gave John, the courage and strength to stand under the Cross of Jesus as it is planted in the sufferings of my life.

Prayer: Lord Jesus, purify my heart so that I may prayerfully participate in every celebration of the Mass to which I go. May my communion with you truly be a holy communion, where the new, abundant life of the Holy Spirit flourishes and bears much fruit. May my life praise you as I become more and more what I receive in the Holy Eucharist.

Heart of Jesus, present in the Most Blessed Sacrament,

I offer myself with you for the salvation of all.

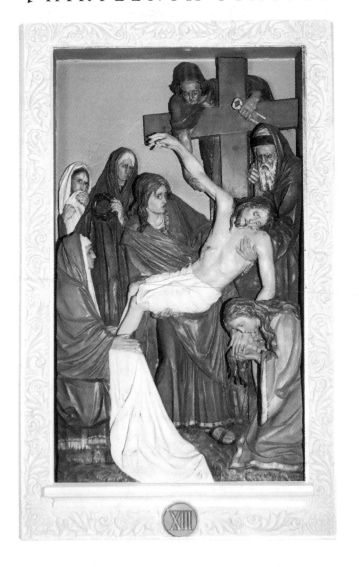

XIII

Jesus' Body Is Taken Down from the Cross

And hope does not disappoint, because the love of God has been poured out into our hearts through the holy Spirit that has been given to us. For Christ, while we were still helpless, yet died at the appointed time for the ungodly. Indeed, only with difficulty does one die for a just person, though perhaps for a good person one might even find courage to die. But God proves his love for us in that while we were still sinners Christ died for us.

Romans 5:5–8

I adore you, O Christ, and I bless you,

Because by your Holy Cross you have redeemed
the world.

The lifeless body of Jesus is taken from the Cross and placed into the hands of his mother, Mary. She holds fast to him before he is sealed in a tomb. I hold what seems to be simply a lifeless wafer of wheat. Yet eyes of faith tell me that there is abundant life here. I need not leave Mass or adoration disappointed. The time spent here may seem so unproductive, so insignificant. But I come here out of love for him who has loved me so much as to die for me.

How disappointed I get when I invest myself in something that goes bad. My heart experiences frustration and maybe even anger when time and effort are wasted.

Jesus invested thirty-three years of life in a project that yielded very little visible fruit. Jesus gave himself completely in doing the Father's will. His words and actions flowed from a heart conformed to the will of the Father. He lived and died to communicate the merciful love of God to us. Jesus' efforts were met with misunderstanding, ingratitude, indifference, and even outright rejection. He must have felt most hurt by those who knew him best yet refused to trust him completely. He depended upon those followers to carry on what he began, yet their hardness of heart stifled their response. How does Jesus react when I ignore or remain unchanged by his love that he offers to me through his Body and Blood? I promise not to lose heart or become discouraged.

Prayer: Lord Jesus, your lifeless body reminds me of the effects of sin. Sin leads to death. Help me to rediscover your love for me, proven by your death. Open my heart to receive your gift of mercy poured out to bring new life and joy.

Heart of Jesus, present in the Most Blessed Sacrament,

I offer myself with you for the salvation of all.

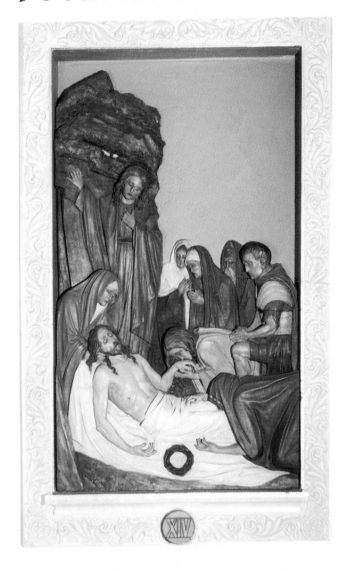

Jesus' Body Is Placed in the Tomb

Jesus said to them, "Amen, amen, I say to you, unless you eat the flesh of the Son of Man and drink his blood, you do not have life within you. Whoever eats my flesh and drinks my blood has eternal life, and I will raise him on the last day. For my flesh is true food, and my blood is true drink. Whoever eats my flesh and drinks my blood remains in me and I in him."

John 6:53–56

I adore you, O Christ, and I bless you,

Because by your Holy Cross you have redeemed the world.

Death. Silence. Tomb. God is silent. Jesus' life on earth is complete. I wait patiently for God to stir. He waits. He wants the death of his only Son to sink in. No denial, no ignoring the truth. Jesus' lifeless body in the tomb reminds me of the cold, dark, stark reality of death. I must spend time contemplating the silent tomb, death's home. Jesus died for love of me.

Jesus never regretted anything he did because he acted and spoke with full integrity, a unity of body, mind, and spirit. He surrendered everything to his Father's will and lived in union with the mind and heart of the Father. Jesus' heart was fully at peace with his Father's heart.

I follow Jesus to the tomb to offer my heart to the Father. I trust not in my own power but in the power of love coming from the Eucharistic Heart of Jesus.

The tabernacle is a place wherein lies the Body of Christ. But this Body is not lifeless. Here I find the One who died and was buried and who rose. He is alive for me today. He comes to me in the Eucharist so that, even though I die and am buried, I will have life and, like him, rise again. I am "ready to wait patiently to hear his voice and, as it were, to sense the beating of his heart" (St. John Paul II, *Mane Nobiscum Domine,* 18).

Prayer: Lord Jesus, you are the humble and Just One who, while fully aware of human weakness, never despaired.

You did not allow the tomb to have the final word. Though you never sinned, you willingly experienced the effects of sin and evil, human weakness, and blindness to truth. You never allowed disappointment or frustration to diminish your trust in the Father. Help me to believe in the power of God's grace to overcome all human weakness. Help me to believe that by receiving you in the Eucharist I will triumph over death.

Heart of Jesus, present in the Most Blessed Sacrament,

I offer myself with you for the salvation of all.

Concluding Reflection

The human body is sacred. God saved us in and through a human body. This human body was not "pre-fabricated" in heaven. No, it was truly of the earth and returned to the earth only to be raised up in order to open for all humanity the path God intended for us from the beginning of creation.

Faith, hope, and love all reside in the human heart. Jesus' heart, sacred and pure, was so totally conformed to the will of God that it embodied the seeds of eternal life, which were poured out in every thought, word, and deed of Jesus. Jesus' whole life was a living sacrifice of praise, a pouring out of himself in love of God and humanity.

In my meditation on Jesus' Way of the Cross, I try to relate my own struggles and sacrifices to the suffering Christ. This happens through prayer. When I pray, I make present in my memory all the sacrifices of my day and unite them to the offering of Jesus' heart in Holy Mass. In this way, my prayer can change the world.

> Prayer joined to sacrifice constitutes the most powerful force in human history.
>
> St. John Paul II